BLOOD VINYLS

BLOOD VINYLS

POEMS

YOLANDA J. FRANKLIN

Anhinga Press
Tallahassee, Florida 2018

Author Photograph: KLJII/ElDot Creative
Cover Image: Photograph — © Dr. Ernest C. Withers, Sr. courtesy of the WITHERS FAMILY TRUST
Design, production: C. L. Knight
Type Styles: titles set in Hoefler and text set in Adobe Caslon Pro
Library of Congress Cataloging-in-Publication Data
Blood Vinyls — First Edition
ISBN — 978-1-934695-57-9
Library of Congress Cataloging Card Number — 2018930156

Anhinga Press Inc. is a nonprofit corporation dedicated wholly to the
publication and appreciation of fine poetry and other literary genres.

For personal orders, catalogs, and information, write to:

Anhinga Press
P.O. Box 3665 • Tallahassee, Florida 32315
Website: www.anhingapress.org • Email: info@anhingapress.org

Published in the United States by Anhinga Press
Tallahassee, Florida • First Edition, 2018

For My People, My Family

For Jeffrey and Brittany

Contents

TRACK III

TRACK IV

Acknowledgments

I am grateful to the editors of the following journals and anthologies in which earlier versions of these poems first appeared:

Apalachee Review: "Half Burly & Bright"

Tallahassee Magazine: "Florida's History of Hurricanes"

Hayden's Ferry Review: "My Controversy" and "Truth Be Told"

College Language Association Journal: "In Miracle of the Black Poet"

Tagvverk Online Literary Magazine: "Just as Hate Knows Love's the Cure," "The Crevice Under Cig-arrest," and "The Desperate Housewife Blues"

Dogwood: A Journal of Poetry and Prose: "Camera Lucida"

IthacaLit: "White Room Syndrome" and "She Ain't No Cindy Lou"

Southern Humanities Review: "Florida Coven"

Political Punch: The Poetics of Identity Anthology: "If Trees Could Talk"

Cave Canem Anthology: "Katrina Conjures Gumbo"

Fjords: Black American Edition: "Climaxes & Joints"

It Was Written: Poetry Inspired by Hip-Hop: "Elegy for Shawn: Omega B-boy Stance" and "Bottom Feeders"

Pluck! Journal of Affrilachian Arts & Culture: "Manual for Still Hunting White-tailed Deer in a Gated Community" and "American Kennel Club"

Squaw Valley Community of Writers' Review: "Southern Girl Hymn"

Journal of Pedagogy, Pluralism and Practice (Lesley University): "Blurry Vision" and "No One I Know Alive Today Was a Slave," "American Kennel Club"

The Infoxicated Corner: "If Trees Could Talk"

Burntdistrict: "Katrina Conjures Gumbo"

African American Poetry Review: "Bop: 40 Acres & a Mule on Apalachicola National Forest"

PMS: PoemMemoirStory: "Vindictive Grace"

Kweli Journal: "Blueprint for Leaving a Black Man" and "Paint Brushes & Booze: 8-Track for Uncle Kent"

Sugar House Review: "Mountain Laurel Blush," "Grave Sight," and "Nutbush Ragdoll"

Saw Palm: Florida Literature and Art: "Florida's History of Hurricanes"

Crab Orchard Review: "Ode to Southern Pot-stickers" and "Where the Dixie Flag's a Tail Light"

SPECS: Journal of Arts & Culture: "Mnemonic Vices" and "Mask-a-Scare"

The Sugarhouse Review: "Porch Sitters Sippin' Sweet Tea in Heaven"

Several of these poems were written with support from the Callaloo Creative Writing Workshops, the Cave Canem Workshop/Retreat, Colrain Manuscript Conference, the Florida State University Creative Writing Program, McKnight Dissertation Fellowship sponsored by the Florida Education Fund, Lesley University, the Millay Colony for the Arts, the Postgraduate Writers' Conference, Squaw Valley Community of Writer's Poetry Workshop Leaders, and the Archie D. and Bertha H. Walker Foundation Scholarship Fine Arts Work Center.

Thank you ancestors. Thank you God. Thank you Kristine Snodgrass and the entire staff at Anhinga Press for believing in and publishing this collection — the soundtrack of my life.

Shout-outs to my comrades at Callaloo and Cave Canem. Thank you to the faculty, staff & writers at Florida State University, especially the following professors: David Kirby, Maxine Montgomery, Jerrilyn McGregory, Rhea Estelle Lathan, Alisha Gaines, Ravi Howard, Virgil Suarez and Maxine Jones. Thank you, Janet Atwater, prayer warrior, for your unwavering support of this project. Thank you, Adrienne Stephenson.

A special thank you to the Get Down Crew at Florida State University: Alex Brickler, Maari Carter, Candace Daymond, Lamar Garnes, Tanya Grae, Jeff Hipsher, Janise Hudson, Janelle Jennings-Alexander, Kenneth L. Johnson, Steve Lapinsky, Kendra Mitchell, Dustin Pearson, Janine Price, Jodi Price, Esther Spencer, Nick Sturm, and Cocoa Williams, for your ride or die wealth of friendship.

Thank you to all of the faculty whose mentorship during my time at Lesley University helped shape this project. Thank you to all of my friends and classmates at Lesley University. A special thank you to Karin C. Davidson, Dom Mattos, Lauren Norton, Laura Polley, Nano Taggart, and Natalie Young.

Love and thanks to every reader in every workshop who has ever offered feedback. Gratitude also goes to the following teachers and friends for commenting on this book or its poems at various stages of development: Chris Abani, Vidhu Aggarwal, Michelle Makalani Bandele, Michelle Courtney Berry, Malika Booker, Dexter Booth, F. Douglas Brown, Drea Brown, Nikia Chaney, Don Mee Choi, Ms. Lucille Clifton, Aaron Coleman, Kristiana Colon, Tameka L. Cage Conley, Geffrey Davis, Tyree Daye, Alyss Dixson, Natasha El-Scari, Naomi Extra, Jennifer Falu, Nikky Finney, Vivee Francis, Daisy Fried, Lisha Garcia, Kiala Givehand, Monica Hand, Kelly D. Harris, Robert Hass, Terrence Hayes, George Higgins, Joan Houlihan, Angela Jackson, Gary Jackson, Galway Kinnel, Yusef Komunyakaa, Li-Young Lee, Robin Linn, Cynthia Mack, Maya Marshall Celeste Guzman Mendoza, Harryette Mullen, John Murillo, Sharon Olds, Gregory Pardlo, Willie Perdomo, Justin Phillip Reed, Ionie Richardson, Magali Roy, Sonia Sanchez, Tim Seibles, Evie Shockley, Chris Slaughter, Jan Smith, John Warner Smith, Patricia Smith, Jane Springer, my favorite cousin MeShun Vann, Laura Swearingen-Steadwell, Amber Flora Thomas, Caroline Randall Williams, L. Lamar Wilson, C.D. Wright, Kevin Young, and Matthew Zapruder.

Thank you to the Callaloo Workshop crew: Ebony Chinn, McKendy Fils-Aime, Nabilla Lovelace, Ciara Miller, Jessica Lanay Moore, Najee Ritter, Clint Smith, Diamond Sharpe, Jennifer Steele, and Charlene.

Thank you to everyone whose names I unintentionally missed here. Know, from my heart, I am grateful. Thank you to Lisa Sgro, my best friend and first reader, and my chosen family, the Sgro-ettes. Thank you to my children, Jeffrey Keith and Brittany Reychel, who save my life every day. To my family: thank you for your love and stories.

Thank you, daddy for passing down your love of music — this foundational chord I now perform as a variation in repetition in homage to you.

 TRACK I

It is a dangerous thing to forget the climate of your birthplace.
— *Judith Ortiz Cofer,* "El Olvido"

Music, at its essence, is what gives us memories.
— *Stevie Wonder*

Elegy for Shawn: Omega B-Boy Stance

1.

Black people love hip-hop!

Ever see a b-boy battle? I've got a burn scar from a cardboard breakdancing mat on my inner
right knee.

We make millions dubbing tracks for white folks.

Well, not millions for each of us, but you know what I mean.

A relevant definition of commerce: when Blacks make money from white folks enhancing
(t)heir rhythm.

Urban Legend: a cardboard break dancing mat will remain portable. Wasn't true, so Shawn
requested an 8X8 linoleum one for his thirteenth birthday.

2.

Boys, boys, boys.

Every summer I had to fight: Gerald, Wendell, that big-ass-kid who stole that purse that Gamma made
me carry. The counterbalance of his tone arm spun like a slingshot double-dutch-tempo. Damn, I
couldn't get a punch in; couldn't equalize control.

My battle record of copper pennies, twin scabs on my knees, reopened, bled down my shins faster
than I could belt-drive away on one of their Huffy bikes.

Huffy bicycles are for boys; domestics are for girls.

Turntables: have you ever wondered why *Home*land Security isn't an office run by girls?

3.

Our Gamma didn't have a Maytag dryer. Since the summer I turned twelve, Tasha and I pinned
the line to dry.

Double-wide = poverty.

Out North Ridge Road, Aunt T lived unhitched, in a double-wide like Gamma, but with cable
and *Yo! MTV Raps*. Shawn used the remote control as a crossfader, channeled our
commercial conversations to a cappella.

Poverty = inherited heirloom.

Gamma died in hers: Parliaments lit like birthday candles inhaled her. Aunt T hitched, inherited
a brick house on Nancy Drive.

4.

Nancy Drive's yard, the square footage of an LP, fade to the church congregation in chrome-
camellias under a mourner's tent once used as shade for front-yard barbeques.

Aunt T: a scratched album cradled by Uncle Michael in the milk crate frame of the doorway.

Blueprint for Leaving a Black Man

I'm a new pair of eyes every time I am born.
— Tina Turner

Ike hit Tina, and then she hit him solo. Debut:
the brink of a platform boot in the backseat

of a limo scene. Ms. Turner left that black man;
her name and Autumn weave split, *You know you love him,*

but can't understand why he treats you like he do when he's such a good man.
1984: Tina, *can't stand the rain … against her window*

brings back sweet memories/ Oh, pain, don't you remember?
The a cappella arabesque of a "Proud Mary," so low

Buddhist rosaries confessed a Hail Mary of catcalls
caused by her fishnet's duet with a denim mini?

Let's skirt:

Ike called back. Sometime after midnight, he wanted
to re-rehearse stage positions again. He agreed

that he looked great right there next to Tina holding
his bass guitar & afro pick, then shouted, "*You better be good to me!*"

My husband, too, held a six-shooter to my head.
I negotiated what love's got to do with staying,

our asleep children, nestled like toes
in peek-a-boo stilettos & that scratched

vinyl of night looped *I'm a soul survivor*
the night I became queen.

Manual for Still Hunting White-tailed Deer in a Gated Community

found poem for Trayvon Martin

Deer hunting in Florida is as old as recorded history.
Actions delineated here are designed to ensure public desires

for recreation. As deer populations grow, so does popularity
of hunting for recreation. The exploitation of deer increases

during this period. "Still Hunting" is characterized by stalking
or concealing oneself and waiting for quarry. The practice

of hunting at feeding stations was legalized, enhancing
opportunities for still hunters to locate and harvest.

In vehicles while coordinating movements with cell phones,
hunters hunt larger blocks, sit next to trees or hide in bushes.

The newly formed Florida Fish & Wildlife Conservation
Commission recognizes the need for public hunting

lands, so Florida's acres are open to public hunting, the vast
majority open to deer hunting. To provide landowners with tools

and flexibility to control deer numbers, the Commission
implemented a deer depredation program. Overpopulation

is the most pressing challenge. Deer in Florida are considerably smaller.
In Florida, whitetails are known to have various types of trauma,

and are a species of wildlife whose over-abundance degrades
its own habitat as well as the habitats of others. Delaying

harvest of bucks until maturity carries rewards: more bucks
in subsequent years and seeing bucks is a key component

of hunter satisfaction. Seminole County is infested
with white-tailed deer, so legislation approved deer eradication

throughout south Florida. Managing hunter satisfaction
enhances overall recreational experiences. The Commission began

the comprehensive surveillance program to occur at two levels:
passive and active. Passive involves observation and culling

of free-ranging deer that demonstrate abnormal behavior
(suspect or target animals). Active includes random investigating

of hunter-harvested deer. The challenge will be to provide
an array of opportunities that deer harvest will continue

as a necessary and desirable practice for many years. Whether
a hunter prefers to harvest only mature bucks, or chooses

to harvest any deer within range is a value judgment.
It is considered the most popular game in Florida.

Florida Coven

Not sure I'm strong enough to cast this spell, but Marie Laveau entrusts her to "wear the crown of power," séance, gumbo, etouffé and a blanket of snakeskin to Zora, a Florida girl too, drenched in light, baptized by gulf tides, a conjurer who can *make a man come home* and recipe gris-gris *to rule the man you love*, so no surprise they're no real borders in the play *Fences*, yet it usurps female runes from Tallahassee, my birthplace. The lineage of Florida women grow chicory roots, so no surprise Angela Bassett's cast as Marie Laveau re-conjures the ancestral narrative of our American horror story, so then I am a conduit-mulatto, one of the first skeleton keys created by a Bajan blacksmith with Cherokee brows, a Florida gal from a coven — women, *grown right up out the ground* with hips as wide as the Okeechobee, so no surprise every man I've loved falls entranced, still ponders what it means to miss Tallahassee.

Blurry Vision

Tallahassee, FL Summer 2002

I remember buying a fresh bunch of collards
on Orange Ave. — green as usual. I was home,

visiting mama with the kids that summer,
running errands from my daughter's to-do-list.

First, I drove by the roadside makeshift produce
stand, then I made a U-turn, parked on the shoulder

behind the tail end of the red pickup truck's full bed
of locally grown crops. I squint for a clearer image

of the smoky, brown eyed man in the slate grey suit's
features, but time has shined a spotlight on the center

of your head. Baldly, right next to you, Daddy, I purchase
green turnips as your eyes square towards me — familiar,

the way the elderly recall time. (Now, I am the iris out
of focus). I squint. You don't even notice who I am.

Bop: 40 Acres & a Mule on Apalachicola National Forest

He left: deep-rooted pecan trees, arms full of hanging moss,
backdrop the eavesdrop of soughing trees near cornfields,
where sweet potato & tomato gardens border remnants
of a rusted fence, the color of dried blood once used to pin
a wayward bull my daddy & his brother taunted on walks home
past the cottonmouth basking on Grandma Lacie's cement doorstep.

you had better hush, hush, hush   Somebody's calling my name

I always jumped or rode over snakes with the front wheel
of my Huffy bike. Daddy pulped bullet grapes or muscadines
for moonshine in the mudroom shot-off from the garage, taught me
how to wade out of quicksand, catch catfish with bare hands
while squatting in shallow pools of fresh water,
& how to track deer, bear, wild boar & the Thanksgiving turkey,
& how to pick blackberries, & plant a strawberry garden atop the hill
where a seven-foot rattler interrupted five brothers with shotguns.

hush, hush, hush   Somebody's calling my name

Could thunder have caused the earthquake grandma Lacie
said loosed floorboards & rattled her photo with the picture
frame lamp of President Kennedy, the same summer I willed
folded washcloths to levitate over the laundry basket
like butterflies caught in a mason jar? The ghost of my great-
grandfather, John Wyart Hill, called my name nightly in psalm.

you better hush, hush, hush   Somebody's calling my name

Drag Queen Bingo, Sarasota, FL

for Savannah & Beneava Fruitville

One of you straight bitches is gonna fuck-it-up!
Now, let's go over the rules: One: Play only

one card at a time & wand your bingo daubers, sluts!
Remember, cheaters will be blown out of proportion.

Two: When you win, yell; "*I*'m cum-ming!"
Three: You can win in a straight line.

Four: When you hear the "special number"
raise your arms above your head & form

the most perfect *O*. Be the ballerina you always knew
you could be & yell: "*O*hhh … sixty-nine!"

All players must fake their best orgasms for free
Jello shots. "Oh, hell naw! Y'all lesbians are late!

We don't repeat the rules & we don't repeat the numbers!"
Five: *B* is for Bitches who run late to Drag Queen Bingo!

If a DOG is called — a delay of game, because one of us
Queens dropped one of our blue balls, it'll take a few

minutes to sniff & recover. Any volunteers?
I means I got it in your eye! *N*40 minutes I'll be in you!

Six: Please know that we will break between
games & when we do, we order one *slippery dick*

before each *cum shot*, blow the busboy before two
cigarettes — then drag down our hoses to wee.

Double Dutch Bust

Wanna hear some grown-up shit? He locked up,
got forty-five for false imprisonment,
and aggravated assault. I solely parent while
that pantomime on furlough eats for free.
He forced a double-barreled curling iron *there,*
where he came. The power cord ain't long
enough to serve his outlet, he enters me instead,
holds a six-shooter hostage against my frame,
clutches me and pillages our waterbed's sheets.
Prisoners, our shadows furnish the living room,
as heavy hips compass his junk inside me.
It didn't make the news. mama said the other
girl was nearly beaten from her life.

She Ain't No Cindy-Lou,

Academy Awards, 1955
(for Dorothy Dandridge)

Picture pixyish Hollywood actresses, figurines
with white-gams & stilettos, white-blonde coifed figurines

with brunette brows. No shabby-chics, glams in gems, couture.
A mink parasitic beauty, framed by white figures

in ermine stoles, chiffon, & crinoline. Cameras
flash, charade voyeurism, halo figurines

They're six, vixen frames front row in boas, fidgeting
in their seats. An irresistible, salient feature

amidst Grace, Ava, Judy, Jane & Audrey, a dolled-
up Dorothy interrupts the cliché — this feat assures

fixated doe-eyes dazzled as powdered noses can-
opied picnic red pouts. Postures erect, gloved fingers

crossed as eyelashes applauded cheekbones. They curtsey,
cut teeth on a black diamond's sepia flesh. Figured,

without demure, some glib glam on the periphery
initiates a whisper about a *Jet* feature:

"Should Negroes Leave Mississippi?" An alcove tainted
by the tabooed fruit of estranged & opal features,

yet she's no shrinking Violet. Without explanation
                                                    she figures,
If I were white, I could capture the world.

Just as Hate Knows Love's the Cure

for Lisa D.

i.

Until recently, I'd never seen an episode of *The Sopranos*. Here, I'll wait while you get over the shock, insert this line break and tune into this episode of *Nurse Jackie* starring Edie Falco's blond locks, a sort of femme-fatal-Italian-machismo. A vehement queen hammers her ring finger in order to hide her affairs & Easter Bunny ability to smuggle prescriptions of pastel pinks & blues to snort, chew, & swallow while I placed your peccadillos of primrose yellow narcissus in a vase.

Know through all your joy and pain/that I'll be loving you

always

ii.

As a nurse, I'll never know why your own creeds ignored the Hippocratic Oath. Even in the yellow Tinkerbell nightgown, secrets you kept were well-hidden eggs only parents would find the morning after the hunt. Back then, over coffee & cigarettes, I wish I knew a spell to undo the curse of our malignant friendship. Would it have been as simple as a sprinkle of Roundup® to get rid of the weeds?

You can rest your mind assured/that I'll be loving you

always

iii.

I promise we'll dance all night at *Harpo's* after you snort coke before bingo, even if your throbbing femur prevents standing. I believe the heating pad cured denial & pacified the illusion of a painful period or was it a pulled hamstring as you slept through the night. We'll still order *Steak-n-Shake* burgers in drive-thru, slurp what's southern about sweet tea & silence what's supreme about secrets while your femur erodes from breast cancer through the night.

Did you know that true love asks for nothing /her acceptance is the way we pay/

that I'll be loving you   always

A Love Bizarre: a Left-handed Golden Shovel Ghazal

after Sonia Sanchez

Since this trouble man's slow dig in my sugar ditch, I concocted a roux,
I made a seafood gumbo from scratch for him — with a hex concocted roux.

I gather up an absolute tolerance of onion, garlic, thyme, &
each sound. I add filé, paprika, butter & flour to clot the roux,

you left behind. Tomatoes simmer into a vermillion stew, I steep
and stretch them: a nylon sachet chock-full of Creole metacarpal runes

on our bed. Cast all my grandmas' double l's: Stella & Isabella
each nite, & some hairs he left in the tub & spit sigils to seal the ruse.

I breathe you with a little salt & a lime I later bury bloom down
(& become high) in soil I transport from St. Helena. You'd grue

if you only knew I walk with ghosts. *If* he only knew I fed
him what I would not swallow — the savory gush in his roux

was his own jism because he's a two-timing, no diming
man & we *can't make it sugar,* you ain't *playin' by the rules.*

Desperate Housewife Blues

The sifted dust of nuptials falls as lightly as powdered sugar

on beignets onto his starched collars & lapels, as filters of stiff,

ornery grounds of *Café du Monde* sag in room corners. A *Tiffany-blue*

litter box of dog collars lies like diamond apology-chokers, &

indiscretions hold hotel receipts the way magnets on the steel face of a fridge

clutch grocery lists for ordained pantry contents. While an aerosol of waist

management boils under an eggshell chandelier, Moulin *Rouge* lipstick

sharpies the family calendar filled with pushpins tacked

over ecru, cratered walls plastered with the stench of boredom,

Lavender & vanilla *Arm & Hammer* suffocates the stiletto-strewn carpets.

The wry grins of vacation photos fixate on lint rollers rottened

by mildewed promises as Big Mama Thornton whines *love's got a hold on me,*

baby, feels just like a ball & chain deafens the daffodils & African Violets on the sill.

"No one I know alive today was a slave"

a response to a Facebook comment

If someone abducted your family,
affected your present
with an infectious amnesia,
then erased your past
for pure sport of profit,
then forced you to bend
like a scarlet ibis, slaved
to pick the South's tropical snow —
       the offspring
from Earth's womb, begging
not to be orphaned, but to be
nursed, begging not to be
last on its crucifix,
a surrogate to history,
whose urgency profits only
white faces — I ask
what to tell a family
still forced to bow?
I tell them
to "cotton on."

 TRACK II

White Room Syndrome

After the poet, Kenneth Goldsmith, read the St. Louis County autopsy report of Michael Brown, the teenager killed by police in Ferguson, as a poem at the Interrupt 3 Conference at Brown University in March 2015.

Preamble

White room syndrome is the white piece of paper facing the author or a clear and common sign of the failure of the author's imagination.

I. Habeas Corpus

Isn't an autopsy report always a eulogy? Especially when the autopsy of a black body is read aloud for "unpoetic effect" to indifferent white academics attending a poetry reading on an ivy league campus *and* the genitalia of a Black body is still the last line. When a white male poet performs as medical examiner and slave owner at an auction block, does the audience become the body?

II. Forensic Report

An autopsy report is almost never read as a eulogy. It is always the salt that wakes the dead in hopes of scaring away the funeral. I clenched my uncle Sonny's hand because my body hung over the edge of a cliff during my cousin Shawn's funeral. A trail of salt ruined my makeup. I tried not to get snot on his hand. I can still hear my aunt's distress from the loss of her only son while dressing his only daughter for his funeral. When these audience members were interviewed, did they have stories that they need interpreters for or maybe the seats were just rows and rows, and empty rows of coffins?

III. Eating the Other

Does the eulogy become Ekphrastic or something like a resurrection? Perhaps we should imagine the catalogue of the Library of Congress's transcripts of the live tweets. I can hear Julius Fucik's "Entry of the Gladiators" over another impossible culpability. Call it poetry, work, art, avant-garde, uncreative neo-racism or necromancy. They will take the body again and again and again.

Black Writer

after Tony Hoagland's "White Writer"

Historically, this donkey gospel's been a partition created
                                     since constitutions.

It's been perceived that our persona eats multiple servings of well-seasoned turnip greens

and that we receive welfare checks at the first of every month.

Nevertheless, we like being identified as Black, as writers.

Has this made it more difficult for us to publish?
                                     Rhetorically, so.

But we can't "get tired" until we publish in White-
                         Only magazines!

When I visit the shanty shelves of the African American Literature section of the bookstore,
                                     how do I feel?

I know that more of us write, write about more than just being that.

Political scandals, intrepid divorces, dying parents;

I know Black readers too need to see their lives reflected on the page —
              (re)memory and vinyl; the fear of vanishing.

The job of the artist is not to leave you where she found you:
this art requires gentrification.

Subsequently, you will start to feel like the rite of blanket clichés
                         are all you'll ever right in this world.

And gradually,
throughout the picketing for

        contentions coloring who you are

you deflect it, it adumbrates you to write *wh*iter, I mean righter, and righter.

Climaxes & Joints

After leaving the parlor, my ink still bleeds pomegranate
sunrise over *you your own best thing* onto the inner hem
of my white cotton-blend tee. Maari smokes

Marlboros 'cause she can't stand the length of history
it takes to smoke the *American Spirit* Jodi offers
her on our sidewalk break. Second-hand smoke

feels up my cleavage & greets customers like the fury
of a Tiger Woods' fist pump, catches the raven-
haired boy with bangs in a Doors t-shirt & skinny

jeans off guard in front of *Osakas,* where I frequent &
order jasmine rice with ornately painted chopsticks —
the kind my sister Lisa likes to stab into her imperfect "Love

is a Racket" red bun. I'm totally into OPI® nails &
Pureology hair since my boyfriend Juan, a poet from L.A.
who used to DJ at The Moon's Latin Night Sweats, broke

up with me over chicken Yakisoba & salmon shioyaki;
rumor has it, a splinter still prevents him from scratching
vinyl like he used to. Jodi & I still frequent The Moon though.

We crossfade between a joint & a trio of Jäger bombs
just to extinguish my memory of the guttural sounds
of sex we once made. While sitting on the stool

covered with the ordinary-black sweater I bought
that year from The Limited, among neon lights,
the smoke from the fog machine must have hid

my crisscrossed chopsticks, those extra appendages —
flicking Juan off, a memento tattoo of a bass line
joint's holler & beat-breaking his final climax.

Camera Lucida

after Frank O'Hara

The cinema is as cruel
as an effigy. We all
perform in the great
art of light and shadow
interrogating everything
about every atomic
inverted projection.
When suddenly a black
Swan appears like what
magic pinholes in a pic-
ture box obscures, there's
panic. *Always by the hand*
that holds the pen. There's
always a message inside
the vulnerability of our
exposure. And isn't the
camera-eye's white eye
reason alone to acknow-
ledge that its reels can only
be illuminated by vetted
darkrooms? Sophomore
year, Chris Heil broadcast
to our history class that
he is the great grand-
son of Oppenheimer.

Oh, how history forgets
its own eidetic memory
like *something so beautiful*
as the radiance of a thousand
suns became the destroyer
of worlds.

Suicide: An Addict's Hymnal

She laid her burdens down, offered God ransom: her soul, a note inserted into an empty bottle of vodka, drained after rallies held in alleyways, walking with lovers, oxygen thieves; she rouletted with needles in her veins, rode the white horse to a place to drown, was tossed and driven, *battered by an angry sea.* She could not sink, so she crashed into boulders and Junk, offered hepatitis B a ride. He hitchhiked her *high*ways, killed her kidneys, now sprites of hallucinations are toms peeping from air ducts. *What a privilege to carry everything to the Lord in prayer.*

The Crevice Under Cig-arrest

1

To clean the exteriors

of homes,

the spider-abductor beaks into webs.

This is what the bird,

outside the bedroom,
on the lanai seems to know.

2

Inside the puff of weed clears.

The weight of life,

Virginia-slims

as the hospice nurse visits

and settles
the angles of death.

3

To the bird,

the southern house

spider suspends,

a patent position,

inside the capillaries
of its victim.

4

In the drywall,
Cancer,

carbon,
a mastectomy

hangs like Van Gogh's
enveloped ear.

5

Spiders never practice
the art of letting go.

Mask-a-Scare

Unnatural locks picket
against bottled-bronze skin
darker than my Cherokee
great-grandmother,
or is she the orange
underbelly of a mango, petite
as a ten-year-old boy? The face,
taut pigskin or latex used
in mass produced horror —
a pinup with scarred temples,
whose hazel eyes skulk
in hollowed sockets for mascara
and a compact's mirror.
Tainted red, pouts the collagen —
lips a protruded requiem.
I'm haunted by how
a monster ended her face,
this permanent
Halloween.

Mnemonic Vices

Lisa, pack your lighter.
The civil war is imploding,
with you the only prisoner!

Life is a shawl stolen
by the Reaper. In your hourglass,
sand has lost its shape.

Hiroshima exhales in your living room
as the mushroom of Hendrix's hedonic haze
hostages *you* Empress, fashioned in new clothes,

flesh-parading, dressed by delusion
in window-view for neighbors.
On the lanai, you dance,

your theater faces: placarded illusions of hope.
Forever is your three-carat diamond ring, not
your escort of Coach purses or museum of trendy shoes —

nor is it your girlfriend's hand,
held during chemo.

Stevie Wonder Sings I Don't Know Why (I Love You) in the Background

Muffled, your acidic,
scolding tone
does not hide facts.

You are at bingo,
the smoke filled palace
of octogenarians

that ogle
the sprite of your beauty,
swiftly stolen

shadows at sunset.
Cancer is an opulent rogue,
the body its mask.

A jackpot is worth more
when players are few.
Fake eyelashes and two-hundred dollar wigs

baldly wear spoils.
Your jeweled fingers —
eyes for leopard's spots,

camouflage your hands.
Age lines your face
like a childhood drawing.

The bingo caller's voice cards time.

Southern Girl Hymn

I come from below the bedazzled belt
of the Mason Dixon line, from a place
where the Florida boot can be seen
as Jim Crow's stiletto. I come from women
who rule Blues men who carry guitar picks
as pacifiers and rub out cigarette butts
like blunts of sage with the same circuitous
notion that a wedding ring does not make
them monuments or placeholders on pot shelves.
I come from women with swollen hands
who create to spite a Parkinson's trimmer
and rogue memory, the sugar, girdled hips
and red velvet laughter luring insulin
the way cat-4 hurricanes sepia gulf
coast skylines, snap its shawl to whip pecan
trees and rustle ratchet wind chimes on wooden
front porches. Where I come from, my South sounds
like pejorative stereotypes, like
the clanging of my mother's aluminum
cake pans, like Trayvon Martin's thank-you-ma'am-drawl
at checkout and Paula Deen's braised remark
to Hollis Johnson, an employee
she asked to her onstage, saying, *He's as black*
as the chalkboard behind me. I come from
magnolias and dogwoods, strawberries and wild
onions, stalks of corn fields and wild acre

peas, muscadine trees and cotton emancipations
of reneged forty-acre deeds — a place,
under a horizon of fickle rainstorms,
where snow only pleads for raincoats, Grandma
Lacie's crocheted hats, and a red-thumbed mitten.
I come from secrets too big to be heard —
a noise so loud angels would swoop and dive
from heaven, where you gotta be
able to either sing "The Battle Hymn
of the Republic" or "Dixie."

Letter to My Boyfriend

A silent qwerty, Palatino Linotype, Times New Roman or Book Antigua
break-up font is less formal than Honey or Dear.

Hey Boo, my Boo, I've stammered over this all day
(no, too formal).
There's something I've been meaning to tell

You. It's not me, it's you. It's all because of you,
all about you. We talk of nothing else if isn't concerning you

Sho! You and your daddy's-baby-maybe-drama must have playbills
In print, delineating the role of each of the characters of your play in one act.

The ink press must be pissed at the number of extras hired to eyeball
each of your soliloquies. No one is listening! Interest owed in full

I'm bored with center stage starring you. How come
I bring a dozen roses every night?

Stiletto, Wedged

        A
Legendary headlights
prowled,

his white baton
— deflated, sticky

from one chocolate
martini,

two buttery nipples
& a salty Senorita.
        B
A pair of olives
arrested him. I was an extra
in the Miranda act.
        C
I fucked him,
slowly seated his lap,

in the backseat,
in the parking lot,

in front of the
nightclub.

He and
the cop
both came.

 TRACK III

Sampling: In Miracle of the Black Female Poet

after Phillis Wheatley, Lucille Clifton & June Jordan

Won't you please come & celebrate with me
> *what she shapes into a kind of life? —*

without a model: both nonwhite & woman
> *a sable Venus whose voyage blesses boats*

that brought her here, & thank whatever
> *gods may be for her unconquerable soul?*

Oh, come & do marvel at how could she
> *sing & know of a lyrical life.*

How did she know & see to be except herself?
> *Come celebrate with me that I am —*

Perhaps, you will because

> *each day something has tried to kill me & failed.*

Florida's History of Hurricanes

after Teresa Cader

Because we cannot know —
we hide dogwood branches used as switches, snap cigarettes sound
        as green-beans, not-knowing
a lighter lures dogs from fields with its flame.

Her papier-mâché-screens surround the house — there's a boxed lit-candle where
banana tree leaves bend next to the master-locked bike shed

where girls weren't allowed.

Gamma's second husband, a strapping man palms a Budweiser,
        escorts her at night through the screened door,

a magnolia tree roots the yard's soot and square-stone tablets
        in the years she lay legless, cancerous,

waiting for the oncologist or endocrinologist, praying. Then

in the season of barren dearth and futility
        it must begin, the season of her casualty.

———◆◆◆———

No southern gospel on the radio, no radio, no choir,
no voices rebuking — no voice — fugue of clotheslines, an eye wall.

Because we cannot know, we imagine

What will happen to us without you?

Most things I remember —

a Category 3 storm pruned oak tree limbs on lawns
in Indian-descent Black neighborhoods.

Uncle Randy threatened to ride his bike like the green Witch
in the Wizard of Oz daring a police officer to write him a ticket for speeding.

Like months of remission —
the eye shifts

The papier-mâché-screens
                are bored behind calm curtains —

and how could she learn to drive after that fire,
a woman who'd never seen brick return to clay?

Downtown the seventh graders in their Bealls' Bermuda shorts
extol, Science rocks. *Black Cloud: The Great Florida Hurricane of 1928.*

We all remember one —

a speeding train, sheets of rain —
                        all indications
that the Panhandle's obsequious hurricane "Kate Amputates Leon County."

———◆◆———

The sky cannot remember its clouding —

around her bed, stolen limbs haunt kneecaps
                still, troubles a pack, hair hot combed Sunday-straight
                        over a gas stove,

urged to slip one between your lips to drag
                yourself from this life in a smoky halo —

I worried you would forget to check
                       the horizon in time.

Katrina Conjures Gumbo

Bayou's kitchen, September 2005

Simmer in a kitchen where the crook of a wooden spoon
often begs for mercy on the burn of an eye. A whole

stick & a half of butter & a teaspoon of flour
blanket the bottom of a skillet the way

naked soles seethe on a rooftop, ripen jaundice
& rhythms in flicks of backlash like mudbugs.

Today's menu — FEMA flew over Marie Lauveau's
X-marked grave. The aerial view over Nola's deep

bowl of surrender-white tee flags look like rice
grains graffiti with black spray paint campaigns,

pungent with rescues & "fuck you's!" Creoles
let off steam in a boiling melody of filé, onions,

in a roux of missing persons & isolated identities.
Their bodies like crawfish sopped in okra & tomatoes,

before a burial in seasoned, soot-rousse — unsolicited
even after the president saw the flipped French Quarter

Say grace *for the nourishment of our bodies, for Christ's sake.*

Ode to Southern Pot-stickers

{Pre-heat}

Let's start with the rib-stickers of waist-wideners that ward off the cold lean of a belly's grumble. Back fat and fat back, with ham hocks, and bacon grease and lard-lined pans — to "season" stews and pots full of vegetables. White acre and black-eyed peas, lima and green beans make tongues live easy and jaws clap in ovation to fill the empty gut.

Let's continue with leftover Thanksgiving's turkey carcass boiled-all-day-down till its spare skeletal frame elbows the pot's brim, and swats at and ducks from the wooden spoon. Just a spoonful of carnage helps the ingredients meld down, in the most traditional way — gumbo, gravy, etouffée, chili, barbeque, roux.

{Main Course}

Vegetarians, like vultures, scavenge too for Earth's tendrils — umbilical fruits, parsnips and organic algae. Southern vegetarians' hands handle oyster knives, cut-up okra and tomatoes, yellow squash and Spanish onions with a teat of brown sugar. Pillagers. Harvesters in-season.

Vegetarians shuck then fry yellow and white corn kernels, strewn with salt and black pepper seasonings. Jiffy cornbread bakes in 9-inch cast iron skillets, coated in vegetable oil. Season-side-up, double-dipped in buttermilk, deep-fried okra drowns paper towels lining a tinfoil cake pan.

{Dessert}

Southerners jar jelly, fill lard-laden piecrusts, patted with flour, and then folded with fruit that's-been-out-all-week. Bananas, apples and pineapples ripen on countertops. Banana puddings, peach & blueberry cobblers meld down with sticks of butter. Cake heaven on holidays, passport us to German Chocolate and Italian Cream; just a slice of cream cheese pound cake, coconut or red velvet, tradition the most Southern way.

Vindictive Grace

In the South
in the Black South

in the Black Southern family
in the church

in the Black church
in the Black Southern church

there are rules:
there's no church without Sunday

no Sunday without school
& no bypass without family

or funerals without menus
or Styrofoam plates of collards,

cakes, & cornbread-hymns
in the Black Southern church

sermons to side pews, where
collections of black ties & hats hum

hands hold popsicle-stick
fans with advertisements & gossip

in Dolby surround-sound where funeral programs
full of picture biography & still so

what if you attended a Black college & studied
Electrical Engineering & then were hired

at Georgia Power & were a member of the union
just to be close so you could drive to visit

your daughter an hour away & only worked
on weekdays & every other weekend

the deacon & pastor will still say there is
no heaven without a church home.

Porch Sitters Sippin' Sweet Tea in Heaven

(Dialogue between Janie Crawford and Pheoby Watson)

Chile, it's not 'bout the water, though love is lak
      de sea. Faults always lift under siege —.
It's 'bout the sex: it's a movin' thing. Katrina
      flaunt her diva complex, but still and all,
her stiletto stilted, & that slut slipped
      her hips over de Big Easy, lap
danced over da Bayou, strut through de French
      Quarter. A harlot in humid perfume
stuck, tugged her girdle, hula-hooped like
      a wooden spoon, while Dixie's sugar spilled,
bystanders stared, an ankle bracelet snagged
      de head of a tombstone. Seduction
rain danced de Creole Sea.
      It was when we was leavin'
or fixin' to consider it
      de first time me and Tea Cake
heart breakin' from da Muck
      back in '28. Dat's whut
'trina act lak a wildebeest
      of a storm lak de one in de Everglades.
The sky had God's handwriting
      in its foreshadows: a sepia photo tinged
wit de rust of waitin.

Girl, look lak Death came through
        there! The horizon kneeled
spirits flood de sky. Watch
        God parade parasols balloon
under the shimmy of Spanish moss shawls.
        Carrions epigraph tombstones.
An insatiable rape submerged de 'glades.
        Uh-huhn, you knowed it too! Spoke
wit dat conjure woman
        who say 'trina left here hurried in a halter-
top, a fiend for Louisiana's
        five-day erection, pining
over some lover: a sultry
        waltz to New O'Lean's moan.

American Kennel Club

In the English Department break room

Over lunch, Becky shares how difficult it is to bury
a thirteen-year old lab. It's two days before Thanksgiving

break. It's my first holiday here in this small town
that shares its traditions of green beans & sweet

potato casseroles, mac & cheese, dressing with all
the fixings, and Turducken. "Tur who?" I ask.

"Is that German? Turducken — a turkey stuffed
with a chicken, stuffed with a duck. I rent

an original Florida home built when Zora wrote
How It Feels to Be Colored Me. My landlord

says the stripped hardwood floors were lain by Crackers,
and brags about how the structure can withstand any storm.

Becky pipes up, "Good news is we found a litter of beautiful
black labs — their mother's a blonde, their father, a chocolate."

Mindy interjects, initiates a sorority of laughter —
"How could *they* litter black puppies?"

If Trees Could Talk

If trees could talk of origins, talk of surnames,
could talk of that hand-tied noose to the anchor

of a gin fan, could talk of hate that spreads
itself as hot-steam froths extra-foam over

the surface of the lip of a cup, so thick, so white,
so creamy over the dark, chicory brew of ancestors

my seventy-four year old mother remembers
as whispers and nicknames of her Grand Bill,

a freedman in Wakulla, undocumented,
yet registered to carry a musket.

I want to hear their voices,
watch them stand, their patinas

a blitzkrieg of revolutionary petunias
set afire Confederate flags

that still hang like Scarlett's draperies
over Florida and Georgia's bloody pastoral

highways, and corners the Mississipppi state flag
like an applause gone with the wind

like a warning of what type of trouble
tends to crop up around here after dark.

There's a Place for Us

after Jessica Lanay Moore

I'm not self-destructive. I am not a person who wants to die.
— Whitney "Nippy" Houston

When you arrive here, you will
with canary, baby chick wings,
flap and onyx
stigmata for feet and sex,
just everything
sucked up in you,
the mouth of your wounds
blades, tongue dry from
what you knew
swallowed up gypsophila,
the flower, your whole body
simple like the legs of scissors.

So, now, my resting
place is left unmarked,
'cause you drowned
swallowing your
whole mouth wide open,
while I learn to be satisfied
here. My satisfaction is a murderer
Bobbi, and wanting you here,
I'm unapologetic —

curiosity can't kill
a black cat in the dark,
we all are baptized with you,

my heirloom. Warded off
debris and unrequited,
your body a black velvet
bag of stones. *It is a curse*
to smell like the wild world —
you cut too much like me,

but we keep our mouths stuffed
with nettle. I let you take
because you knew too
many secrets —
you soaked us up
with what we always
knew.

Someday, my daughter
too will need
sea salts and spider webs
soaked in lavender cradle-
songs to suture that empty
space between casket
and vestibule. When I arrive
will my own selfish longing
for baby's breath summon
her too?

Where the Dixie Flag's a Tail Light

Spite's the hand-
cocked mimic trigger
bound to a cross-
road of stripes & queues
where stars bangle
empty civility's bales
of "hey," no longer
noosed by yessuh's or yessum's,
the ordained order
where Jim Crow's brute
cast-iron, five o'clock shadow
uproots a thigh-high hemline
just below the fabric-
folds where the Mason Dixon
Line's belted skirt warns
of this man whose balls swagger bull
of this man *who has seen*
the change of life.

True, So if You Should Ever Doubt

A weathered pair of grey, sun-licked rockers'
click-clock, paint flaked and faded, sentinels

screened on an original Quincy, FL
porch, face-off and whisper marriage advice

to a visiting grandson & his wide-eyed-
brown-eyed girlfriend. "It's easy if the two

of 'em can get along, but if you can't —
might as well split. But stay together

if you can, if there's kids involved.
Shame when they have to suffer

through. You married?" Papa's
knees point at the one he's shared

this porch with for over forty-years.
Her eyes still glint with loving-sarcasm,

lifts her wrist, turned inward, a confused
command of Parkinson's, her mouth

a twisted Ficus tree, mocking him with her puppet
hand, squawking to break up the familiar-faced,

brown-eyed, wide-eyed girl's interview, whose shock
shimmers as the bronzer on the bridge of her nose

flickers, then equates the comfort of the fifteen-
year divorce to the shade of a magnolia tree,

waits for the grandson, who's outgrown his room
to kneel like branches do against the lure

of ripened grapefruits, a prayer
so loud, fruit flies fan promised pulp.

"You wanna know the secret? It's that
the truth don't need no fixin'. Know why?

Because you ain't got to fix nothing
that ain't already broken. It's that easy."

With dimples and a nod, the grandson
confesses to his Papa that on a curlicue phone

cord, twenty-five years ago, the landline between
long distance phone bills to Tallahassee, he once paid

because of calls to *this* very girl, in the late eighties; reunited
first loves *flashback — almost left behind*, but *the secondhand* rewinds.

Mountain Laurel Blush

for Mary Kay Ash, Founder of Mary Kay Cosmetics, Inc., Dallas, 1968

after Amanda Auchter

They will drive it, she said
when they suggested she change

    her mind, to reconsider

        the topcoat, its nacreous
lacquer. *I know they can be*

all they believe.

        Even the bumblebee
            flies, flouts its aerodynamics.

In this car, she remembers

        the mountain laurel

    blush, her compact blooming
    in her palm. How the pageantry of women

        string alongside like freshwater pearls, waving.

Witness a white boa. A door opens.

        A classic. The Cadillac.
            Her face haloed with blonde,

camera flashes. The pearlescent-pink paint against

its oyster shell interior. And oh, that blush-trophy.

A woman with a set of keys in her hand.

TRACK IV

My Controversy, 1986

Here we are in this big old empty room/staring each other down …
— Prince Roger Nelson

            First time I fell I was thirteen & it
was at the first sight of a shirtless man
            the color of raw & unrefined
shea in a licorice speedo
            handcuffed to his crotch.
I do not want to say
            this controversy was caused
by a Prince poster fixated
            to the closet door of my cousin
Army Greg's record room or
            that a waist chain lassoed his body
beyond the verge of being
            obscene — all of him an offering:
each of his hands raised
            to each side of his temples —
elbows, symbols for greater than all,
            within this tesserae tile shower
frame & that in the background
            a crucifix levitate too.
I do not want to say
            that in this room full of crated albums,
this man's hazel eyes & trojan,
            my blood   began   to spin
                    like a needle   on vinyl
until   my kingdom   come.

Paint Brushes & Booze: 8-Track for Uncle Kent

Memories don't live like people do.
— Angie Stone

Thought everyone had at least one uncle
who's a modern day Staggerlee who pimps

a Kangol & keeps a weed stash in the top
drawer of a nightstand, behind a pearl-handled

pocket knife he once used to shave a man
of his pride, then reused it to pop open the caked

lid of a paint can & flicked the back
of the blade to release the ooze from inside

a Natural Light in his "love shack," built
from beams of condemned houses —

a shotgun scaffold with a tin roof so thin
rain showers sound like gunshots, thick

insulation of peeping toms seeping from faux-
plywood walls to eye wallpaper of *Jet* beauty

centerfolds. I imagined my uncle as the Black Hugh
Hefner, Dolemite reincarnate who drove the white-

ibis '65 hardtop Dodge Dart with crimson interior
my father bartered for refurbishing, in exchange for

the German Shepherds he trained for Tallahassee
PD's K-9 unit, afterhours & on days off from the steady

painting job that left an ash of primer so thick, on marble-
sized knuckles, cocoa butter couldn't quench it. These

same hands extend a blunt rolled airtight out a car window
as a nod of advice, & a squint thru blood-shot eyes led

lifelong lessons on how to master pressure points on my cousins'
hands & neck — an exercise in pain-tolerance carried over

to a good card game of knuckles that'd last as long
as Jackie (his heavy-steady) could tolerate the screams

over her high, which was shorter than the width of their blue-
jean bellbottoms & those sideburns. Send me, shotgun

in that Dodge Dart as the Isleys croon *drifting on a memory,*
ain't no place I'd rather be from the 8-track console.

Grave Sight

Aunt Martha had to bend twice this year, over
      grottos, practice the art of farming

bones, accept Death's polygamy like
      Ojo de Agua's living

Mirabal sister, grit the rigor of fists,
      & cross-stitch a delicate symphony.

Two needles of bodies' cymbal *all the preparations*
      that had to be made. She pined over mahogany,

chose two caskets — one for her only son crushed
      in his Cadillac, bandbox in green;

the other for her youngest brother embezzled
      by asthma — here in the anteroom of *Strong*

& Jones' Funeral Home, a calligraphy of ties
      press the necks of formaldehyde kin.

On the outskirts of my father, I see a God-made anomaly

through lakes large enough to receive with ease the gush of Coltrane's
A Love Supreme. This is a fact: my great-grandmothers always
live past ninety-three & all their husbands, give birth
to more sons than daughters who all, *at one time or another,*
have been told to shutup, don't talk too loud, too slow, or for too long,
in Tallahassee, in the Carolinas, in the Gullah Sea Islands,
& in Wakulla out route 16, & in St. Peter's Primitive Baptist
Church. My father tells me, in his music group days,
during the high reign of Berry Gordy & soul-rock & roll
that men like him were recruited whenever they would roll
into Tallahassee, a small, old town full of abandoned fields.
These men, then, were to commence impromptu jam sessions
& were compensated the perks of *it's a man's man's man's world.*

In spite of this, my father still toted me along with all
his equipment knowing girls, always, are only meant
to be seen, elegant & graceful in manner, appearance,
& shape, & I would surely be scolded if heard recalibrating
the language of my father's digest or even the way he chords
stories from *those small provinces of silence into the kind*
of love that always troubles that silence into music — the first word
I learned for poetry. The South struggles to stretch gentility —
the quietly appealing or polite quality free from vulgarity or
rudeness — taut over my body — a woman's body, my grand-
mothers' Stella & Isabella's bodies, & my mother's body
to mute the ancestor of language wristed by the brassy
jangles of tambourines. I've learned this: My father's aunt married
my mother's uncle, & some of us have been demure fabulists.

For example: Stella, (redacted her first marriage to Jentrus
J. Jackson, & taught me how to clean so I'd know who to fire)
& my mother Dollie (changed her name from Daisy, just like
her mother Stella did from Calla Lea & she taught me how to bury
secrets like her favorite cake recipes in the bottom of the silver-
ware drawer); Isabella Bolden (bartered the wealthy White
surname Lewis from Lewis State Bank, the only bank in the South
to survive the great depression), & Grandma Lacie is one hundred
years old (my father's mother, outlived three sons, two husbands,
& still lives in the house with the lamp lit photo of JFK,
& a working well). Now my father's blues posts under a tombstone
like the last trail marker of the chitlin' circuit. These are not lies.
This is the truth. My family comes from a long line of women
whose heartbeats sound like a needle run out of vinyl.

St. Valentine's Day Massacre

I.

A sepia photo stills life:
an image of Calla Lea

posed, poised, on edge
of a cushioned stool, smoke

escapes your cigarette. Crossed
at the knee, legs dressed

in fishnet hose, you wink.
The b-lined skirt squints

at the cameraman, reel in a school
of beaus with one flash,

a smile hooks, they
squirm-breathless. Decked,

a Captain ordering
all men to see.

II.

She murdered my
grandfather, shot

him glasses of vodka,
fish-tanked him, after

she lured & netted him
in fishnet stockings.

III.

Ain't Misbehavin' hangs
in the foreground. A man

lured to your coy, lyrical
shot, snaps out of his

panting daze. Behind the
camera, he weights a stool

at the bar. You have zip-locked
& bagged this specimen of the sea:

fish-tanked, his glass clears
before you light your next smoke.

Snapshot Cabaret

She balances
a sallow silk stocking
of Lady Nicotine
between the beams

of her ringed fingers.
The garter-belted filter
dances a duet
with her lips.

A chorus line
lines a chorus,
swirls a single
ruby-red slipper

to ash
after a finger flick,
head-tossed drag.

Southern Redactions

No one ever tells the whole story
or the whole recipe, especially
not the women in my family

who rule with cast iron skillets.
Because of the Sundays Gamma
made me the pancakes

her mother made her,
I now return now to the yolks
nestled in brown and cracked

half-shells, one at a time,
split into separate bowls
to avoid spoiled leaks

into creamed butter,
tablespoon all-purpose flour,
batter the history of acrid secrets,

the orange juice, then equal parts
milk. Remember the delicate
rituals, how petite hands uncurl

cold, slimy slabs of packaged
bacon into hot cast iron, so
a charred, crisp-edge forms on the white-fat,

pig-tail curls. Perhaps, the bacon grease
drowns a paper towel sheeted pie tin too.
I marveled at the whisk of Gamma's

wrist: a yellow spatula and ring
the batter in a ceremony of patience,
reticent like the dogwood sentry

blooms on the acres out her kitchen window
in Tallahassee, the Apalachee Indian word
for *old town* or *abandoned fields*.

———————•••———————

I eavesdrop during kitchen baptisms,
overhear how the original house
next to the trailer burned as fragrant

as the hot-comb she used to press our roots
lies on the eye of the stovetop that kept
the ash of Gamma's Parliaments hung-over

that crucial night after cleaning
flesh of fresh-hooked Apalachicola
mullet the color of her trademark lipstick,

and I imagine the gush of blood caused
by the machete my great-grandfather warned
mama not to touch; the gash between

her thumb and index finger that bled until
her grandmother stuffed it with wiry
cotton of a spider's web. The fried fish grease

cooled on oil-soaked slices of white bread.
If only the eavesdrop of leftover sweet
Vidalia onion hushpuppy batter, probably

splashed with beer, and crushed Budweiser
can ashtrays could spill the ingredients
that an eye-measure of milk

and a tablespoon of brown sugar sink
into the kept-on-low cheese grit quicksand,
expose the ingredients of this girl

raised in a South where I sat at Gamma's
kitchen table with my cousin Shawn
and my brother, three canary place settings,

a restaurant ready to receive grace,
sopping like Aunt Jemima's smile.
My grandmother's hands

hung-dry, folded, and straightened
the cuffs of fitted bed sheets,
never learned to drive, pressed

new money as the help for thirty-years.
I replicated those intimate memorials
of rigor and grits with my own hands,

now leaning over a casket to straighten
the lapel on Shawn's black suit and red
tie whisper his name in psalm.

Bottom Feeders

I wore unemployment like a shawl in Florida humidity the day FEMA was an off-duty lifeguard when Katrina lap danced over Nola, received an eviction notice in a section-8 community called Wellington, and survived a car crash in a Geo Prism that left me without the use of my hands for six weeks. The property developers of my apartment complex must have strategically chosen that symbolic meaning of the community name. They must have anticipated the necessity for the tenants to wear *knee-length waterproof, rubber or plastic boots* in order to "pull yourselves up by your own bootstraps," even if you are a Black, educated, single parent of two teenagers, who's been nominated for a Disney® Teaching Award, you're still broke and tread. First thing every morning, in the 3/2 house I rented from a progressive six karats in total daily wear Barbie, I brewed Café du Monde and watched Kanye from the couch say, "President Bush doesn't care about Black people!" — what every American Black was thinking and feeling while I searched for my cousin, a chef on Bourbon Street, and my friend Nelson. It's been three months. I'm still waiting to get foodstamps. Maybe he just cares about bootstraps. Maybe his colorblindness prevented him from seeing people sunbathing on the rooftops of the houses that were treading water like buoys. Maybe he thought that as long as Black people in the Bayou wear Wellingtons, they won't drown! Maybe he mistook them for catfish or crawfish — any native bottom feeders of the sea.

Half Burly & Bright

It started with stolen matches and Uncle Bay's rolling papers. He always purchased the ones that came in a tiny, rectangular box that looked like a linen closet for miniature dolls. The box was slightly longer than the book of matches that also sat on the coffee table next to his leather recliner in the crowded living room full of furniture-so-close-together that the espresso piano could only be played when he carefully removed each of my Aunt Ethel's porcelain tea set pieces from its bench tucked away in a hidden nook. I took two of those rolling papers; thin as the wax paper my mama buries her cake batter so patiently on, to stuff the tobacco from his *Half and Half Burley & Bright* tin can before I could light the twisted wad with dexterity. Not bad. At least another slow drag, I thought, as the self-rolled cigarette tumbled onto the flat-grey carpet. Then those flames of poinsettia leaves demonstrated how fire works. I jumped, stomped, and then shuffled the way Grandma Lacie does in her hand-sewn, polyester-white, during Sunday sermons not knowing that nothing could extinguish the bottom of a boiling-pot sized burn spot or the smell of sin, so I covered it with newspaper and prayer.

Nutbush Ragdoll

a vaudeville gen(i)us narcissus: a Misrepresentation by Be(yond)say(knows)

This R&B action figurine accessorizes both the tattered denim mini & dominatrix-black pleather skirt, popped-collar, acid-wash jean jacket — flesh against an invisible waist &

detachable sex-icon wigs & lace-front lion's mane, switchable fishnets or *Hanes*-her-way nylons in true-to-scale, five-inch stilettos. This triple threat's two shades of mahogany

& pomegranate lips accentuate steel-chrome-microphones, flouts pop, bats false-eyelashes & facsimile-patents the blueprint D-I-V-A in divorcée's *still* tagged Queen

of Legs. Long. of Rock. On. Leans rhythm on heir's thighs. Leans on rock. Oh, what thighs. Walk. Southern city limits. Lone star. Icon. *Re*con: the innovator-hit-re-maker

shimmies gospel. God spells W*hoa* man! Whips her wigs back & forth. *Still!* Choreo-out-performs, every little southern girl's proud-mary-private-dancer, karaoke-dream.

truth be told

      i.

mother, i'm waiting
for you to die so i can tell the story about how on the night my husband tried to kill me
i called to tell you this would happen: my husband, the gun, the rape the gun the dream i had
the night before under the ceiling fan, a metronome of doom like the single sound of a turnstile
playing *what's love got to do with it* on repeat i repeat *help me make it through the night* and you ignored
my premonition while we were held hostage in that house on a four-way stop

      ii.

all i could
remember remember were the Sundays you and daddy played Tina like the secular pray *let's stay*
together but my husband my husband and your grandkids and i and i and i and i and i drove by that house
today on the corner of that four-way stop on the corner of that four-way stop we left i left that corner
of the four-way stop and now i know you had to know had to know how *it takes a fool to learn*
how love don't love now i am a deck full of queens, sentries who *steel claw better be good to me*
and know i know i know i know you still believe that i deserve this soundtrack i live but didn't i
didn't i make you the most beautiful consequences of love?

Bop: Autobiography of a Jukebox or Five Ways to Kill a Gardenia

daddy never beat me   like mama did   she made me bend   between my engorged
      breasts & pregnant   belly over the tub edge   to scrub porcelain white
as a wedding dress   she said, *I ain't never gone be able*   *to wear*   *anyway*   Saturday
      mornings   I removed the ring of sin   made it a virgin   again   beat back nausea & silt
I kilt myself   into exact   prepped folds of cotton   white cloth with *Ajax*
      same way   Gamma donned   domestic work   like reluctant prayer.

I used to beyour stveet mama … but now I'm just as sour as can be

mama got demons in spades   used daddy's black leather   belt one he wore   wherever
      he took me   guess it was pride   or maybe just her version of backhanded
it ain't easy   to admit the Blues   is a woman   a supernatural something
      who carries a clutch   of penance & provocation   in bravado   maybe mama
would tell me   if she could   about life   with/out my father   offer
      more   than a folder full   of forty-year old newspaper clippings
with dog-ears bent   like the edges of Bessie's   blue notes   mama
      tucked   her jealousy   behind her ear   like a gardenia.

Yes, I'm mad and have a right to be after what your daddy did to me

mama folded   to her knees   when her only daughter arched her back in the secular
      name of love   like Janie Crawford   beneath a pear tree   her eyes watching God   &
a dust-bearing bee sink   into sanctums   of blooms   instead of some pulpit & pews
      to line chastity's hem   perhaps the Blues is   a good woman   quiet   as it's kept
      under siege in service of myth to sharpen love in   a nice dry house   perhaps
I just can't imagine   how mama had to bend   into an instrument   never meant to carry her tune.

I used to be your sweet mama sweet papa … but now I'm just as sour as can be

Liner Notes

TRACK I

1. "Manual for Still Hunting White-tailed Deer in a Gated Community"
   A found poem for Trayvon Martin is adapted from the Florida Fish and Wildlife Conservation Commission's "Strategic Plan for Deer Management in Florida 2008-2018."

2. "Florida Coven"
   Lines in this poem have been borrowed from August Wilson's play *Fences*.

3. "A Love Bizarre: a Left-handed Golden Shovel Ghazal"
   A lyric in this poem has been borrowed from track six of Marvin Gaye's soundtrack and twelfth studio album, *Trouble Man* (1972) and lines have also been borrowed from Sonia Sanchez's "Poem #3."

TRACK II

1. "Black Writer"
   A line in this poem was borrowed from Ms. Lucille Clifton.

TRACK III

1. "Sampling: In Miracle of the Black Female Poet" is written in the Cento poetic form.

2. "Where the Dixie Flag's a Tail Light" A line in this poem is borrowed from Zora Neale Hurston's *Their Eyes Were Watching God* (1936).

3. "True, So if You Should Ever Doubt"
   The poem's title has been borrowed from Madonna's song "True Blue," on the album *True Blue* (1986). A lyric in this poem has also been borrowed from Cyndi Lauper's second single titled, "Time After Time" on her debut album *She's So Unusual* (1983).

4. "My Controversy, 1986"
   A lyric in this poem has been borrowed from "Little Red Corvette," the first track on Prince Roger Nelson's fourth studio album, *Controversy* (1981).

5. "Paint Brushes & Booze: 8-Track for Uncle Kent"
   A lyric in this poem has been borrowed from The Isley Brothers' "For the Love of You" track on the album titled, *The Heat is On* (1975).

6. "On the outskirts of my father, I see a God-made anomaly"
   Lines from this poem have been borrowed from Patrick Rosal and Cornelius Eady.

7. "truth be told"
   Lyrics in this poem have been borrowed from lyrics sung by Tina Turner on her albums *Private Dancer* (1984) and *Tina Turns the Country On* (1974). A lyric in this poem is also borrowed from the song "Love Don't Love Nobody" on the album *Might Love* (1975) by The Spinners.

8. "Bop: Autobiography of a Jukebox or Five Ways to Kill a Gardenia"
   Lyrics and lines in this poem have been borrowed from: Bessie Smith's track "I Used to Be Your Sweet Mama," on her title album, *Blue Spirit Blues* (1928), Zora Neale Hurston's Magnus Opus, *Their Eyes Were Watching God* (1936), and Rita Dove's poem "Canary."

About the Author

Yolanda J. Franklin is a Cave Canem and Callaloo Fellow, a recipient of a 2016-2017 McKnight Dissertation Fellowship and a Kingsbury writing award. Franklin is a Visiting Assistant Professor at Florida Agricultural & Mechanical University. Her poems appear in the current issue or are forthcoming in the following journals: *Hayden's Ferry Review, Southern Humanities Review,* and the *Apalachee Review.* Her poetry also appears in the recent anthology "It Was Written: Poetry Inspired by Hip-Hop" and is a two-time recipient of a J.M. Shaw Academy of American Poets Award. Franklin is a third generation Floridian, born in the state's capital — Tallahassee. She loves dancing to old school hip-hop, baking, food tasting, and can be found at her favorite coffee shop, Black Dog Café in Railroad Square enjoying a drink the baristas named after her.